Creating

with the

Floral Classic

A

Step by Step

Guide

Written by

The Horticultural Institute of Southern California

Roxanne DePalma
Floral Styling

Robert and Roxanne DePalma
Book Design and Text

Copyright 1999 by the Horticultural Institute of Southern California

ISBN 0-9673044-0-7

All rights reserved. No part of this book may be reproduced in any form by any electronic or mechanical means, including information storage and retrieval systems, without permission in writing from the publisher. Reproduction in English or other languages prohibited.

Printed in Hong Kong

Magnum (Offset) Printing Company Limited

Published By:

The Horticultural Institute of Southern California

P.O. Box 457

San Clemente, CA 92674-0457

www.floralarranger.com

Introduction

Congratulations on your purchase of our Floral Classic. Whether you are a novice or have experience with flower arranging, working with the Floral Classic will be a rewarding, fun experience for everyone.

The Floral Classic is made for versatility. It consists of three separate units. Two three vase units, and one four vase unit. The units can be stacked, or used in a variety of groupings.

The Floral Classic is dishwasher safe. Simply place the vases upside down on the top shelf of your dishwasher. You can also clean the vases by using a quarter of a tablet of effervescent denture cleaner or vinegar and warm water.

For your convenience, we have designed each page so that each bouquet or appetizer can be easily recreated at home by following the step by step instructions. Have fun with your new vases. Remember, use your imagination, always have flowers around you and you will forever have a beautiful a home.

Tools & Tricks of the Trade

The secret to the perfect floral arrangement in our Floral Classic is to "cut all the flowers the same length."

Scissors-Use for cutting all soft flowers stems and decorative accessory items.

Ruler-Measure your flower stems. Remember the trick is to cut all your flowers the same length.

Wire Cutters-Use on all tough flower stems and naturally on all wire stemmed flowers.

Small Paring Knife-Good for fruit and vegetable preparation, shaving the tough exterior off heavier stemmed flowers and removing thorns from roses.

Thin Spouted Watering Can-Use for easy filling of vases, and daily watering without having to remove the flowers from the vases.

Floral Wire-To reinforce and strengthen thin, delicate or rubbery stems.

Clear Nail Polish-Prevents rusting of stems on silk flowers when mixed with fresh flowers.

Funnel-Used to fill vases with dried anchoring materials, such as silica sand, salt, grits or any dry item that will hold flowers in place.

Most of these items we already have at home. They are easily purchased and are very inexpensive. You will probably discover some of your own favorite tools and accessories.

Elements and What to Work With

Selecting Flowers-Medium size flowers for the bulk of your "feature" flowers balance the vase. Smaller blossoms and greenery should be treated as "filler" flowers and help to round out open spaces and add color contrast.

Length-The most important rule when determining the length of your flower stem is "Cut all the flowers the same length." The longer the stem, the larger the bouquet. Short stems create a compact, traditional bouquet.

Balance-The Floral Classic has taken out the guesswork. In traditional flower arranging, balance is very important. By stacking all three of the Floral Classic units, you will create a perfect circular bouquet. The Floral Classic has been designed so that each vase has been fused together at the proper angle to create a perfectly balanced arrangement every time.

Color-Remember "color" will have the greatest effect on the image or motif that you are creating. To achieve a soft delicate, romantic bouquet, use pastels, soft tints, tones and hues. Pink, peach, cream ivory and beige are examples of pastel colors. For a dramatic theme, use more intense colors, known as Jewel tones. Ruby red, teal green, amethyst purple and topaz gold are examples of this. And a fresh primary bouquet, use red, royal blue and bright yellow and offset the primary colors with white fillers.

Preparation

Fresh Flowers-Fresh and healthy flowers, how beautiful they look is so important. Two key factors to look for:

1. Brightly colored tight blossoms.

2. Strong, straight stems. (Flowers fade as they age, their petals loosen, droop and the stems bend. Not a desirable look.)

Silk Flowers- Silk flowers are less effort but the price range varies tremendously. It might be wise to spend time researching costs and selections. You can really save with silk flowers by purchasing them in mixed bouquets. You get a good variety of flowers and waste is less.

Dried Flowers-The dried flowers vary as much as fresh, and you can dry your own. Remember their fragile make up. Dried flowers require delicate handling. Add a piece of floral wire and wrap with floral tape to reinforce stems. The delicate dried stems cannot be forced into resistant filler. Use non-caking silica sand, salt mixed with rice or hominy grits.

Foods-Select fresh, firm and colorful fruits and vegetables. Cut to desired length. Immerse in cold water to maintain freshness until ready to style the arrangement. Style the final arrangement as close to serving time as possible. Place the greens in water as soon as possible to prevent wilting. Dip fruits and vegetable in lemon juice immediately after cutting and they will remain fresh for hours. Using cold cuts and cheese, place them in your freezers for twenty minutes before cutting. You will make cleaner cuts with them being cold.

Use of Vase

Your "Floral Classic" consists of three separate units. Two three part units and one four-part unit. One of the beauties of the "Floral Classic", use the units separately or all together.

To make your arrangement, fill all your vases. If you are using fresh flowers, use water; if you are using dried or silk flowers, use sand, salt or hominy grits. The most important step that you always must do is cut all your flowers all the same length. Put all your flower heads together, and cut the stems to the desired length. Simply place a flower or two into each of the vases.

Use your "Floral Classic" to root houseplants like ivy. If you have just a few flowers, use just the four-part unit solely and place it on a coffee table or end table. If you have more flowers, make up your both of the three part units and place them on each side of the four-part unit. They can be placed wide apart or grouped closely together.

If you want a round bouquet, stack the two three-part units on top of each other and place the four-part unit on top. You will have a beautiful, professionally designed bouquet.

1. Use all three units of your "Floral Classic" and fill them with water. Stack all the units together.

2. Cut all your flower stems to six inches in length.

3. Place one iris in the top vase. Place one iris in each of the bottom three vases.

4. Add two or three of the white or purple mums to every vase.

5. Add remaining miniature carnations to all the vases.

6. Place your heather and wax flower to fill in voids and to fill in spots. Enjoy!

Silk flowers are nice when you do not have fresh flowers. This is made with pink miniature alstromeria and silk babies breath. Keeping the colors the same gives this fresh bouquet a scent of spring.

1. Use all three units of your "Floral Classic" and fill them with silica sand.
2. Cut all the lilies and the babies breath to seven inches in length.
3. Place one lily stem and two babies breath stem into each vase.
4. With the unit's separated, place the four-vase unit in the center with one vase facing the front. Slide the three-vase units on each side of the four-vase unit. Make the arrangement wider by sliding the tree-vase unit closer together or further apart.

Pink Alstromerias and pink babies breath creates a breath of fresh air with silk flowers.

1. Stack all three units together and fill with silica sand.

2. Cut all the lilies and babies breath to seven inches in length.

3. Place one lily and 2 babies breath stems into each vase.

Enjoy this bouquet on a kitchen table for a brunch or use as an accent for a baby shower.

Spring, fresh flowers and fresh smells.... This bouquet is made with luscious pink Gerbera daisies, white Monte Cristo, purple clover yellow fragrant freesia and maidenhair fern.

1. Use all three units stacked together. Fill your vases with water.
2. Use eight pink Gerbera daisies and cut them to seven inches in length. Place one flower in each of the vases of the four-vase unit. Add the remaining four flower into three part units.
3. Cut your freesia to seven inches in length. Evenly distribute them throughout the vases so the yellow is evenly spread.
4. Cut seven stems of clover seven inches. Distribute the clover in the bouquet.
5. Cut the white Monte Cristo to seven inches in length. Fill in spaces or voids with this filler flower.
6. Add your maidenhair fern evenly throughout the bouquet.

These colors and textures of flowers truly say **SPRING**. This bouquet is made with purple Liatrus, yellow daisy mums, hot pink asters, light purple freesia, and purple status.

1. Use the entire set. Leave the units separated.
2. Cut all your flowers to six inches in length.
3. The top vases of your four-vase unit place your liatrus in. Remember to always strip your stem of any leaves that would touch the water. This helps to keep your water clean.
4. Add one or two daisy's to each vase.
5. Place the pink aster throughout.
6. Add the light purple freesia evenly.
7. Use your purple status to fill spaces or voids.
8. Place the four-vase unit in the center of the table and the two, three vase units to either side.

1. Use all three units. Fill them with water. Leave the units separated.
2. Ten pink baby roses are needed. Cut them on an angle to 5 inches in length. Do not leave them out of water too long or you will have to make another clean cut. Place them in the water.
3. Using one rose at a time, break two or three sprigs of babies breath and wrap around each rose. Remember to cut the babies breath slightly shorter than the rose. This will accent the rose. Place each mini bouquet into the vase.
4. Place the four-vase unit in the center of the table and the two three-vase units.

Rooting plants in your vases is easy to do and they look pretty. This is ivy in the four-vase unit and it will continue to grow for months.

1. Use solely the four-vase unit.
2. Fill with water.
3. Place two or three cuttings into each vase.
4. Change the water and rinse out vases every two weeks to reduce algae buildup.

A bouquet of garden fresh summer flowers.... These gerbera daisies, yellow freesia, monte cristo, hot pink clover show off your gardening efforts.

1. Use all three units. Fill with water.
2. Cut all your flowers to seven inches in length.
3. In the four-vase unit, place one gerbera in each vase. In the three vase units add the remaining four flowers.
4. Add yellow freesia throughout the vases.
5. Add hot pink clover evenly.
6. Fill in with the white monte cristo and maidenhair fern.
7. Place the four-vase unit in the center of the table and the two three vase units to each side.

White miniature carnations, pink roses, yellow yarrow, light purple heather, purple and white monte cristo is what you will need for a summer picnic table bouquet.

1. Stack the entire set of vases. Fill the vases with water.

2. Cut all your flowers to seven inches in length.

3. Use ten pink roses, one in each vase.

4. Add white miniature carnation. Use the buds from the carnation too. They will open up.

5. Fill in with yellow yarrow. Remove all greenery from the bottom two inches of the stem.

6. Add light purple heather throughout the bouquet.

7. Accent with the white and purple monte cristo.

1. Use the entire "Floral Classic."
2. Fill the vases with birdseed.
3. Cut all the flowers to eight inches. Dip all the stems into clear fingernail polish and let dry. This will seal off the bottom of the stem so they will not rust in the vases.
4. Add one ranuculus to every vase. Position the flower to be upright. The birdseed will hold the flower in place.
5. Place one zinnia in each vase.
6. Fill in with the variegated maidenhair fern to fill any voids or holes.

This blaze of color is probably the easiest and most striking bouquet. It is made with silk flowers, but the vases have been filled with water to give the illusion of a fresh arrangement. Rust silk alstromerias is all that was used with a touch of candlelight.

1. Fill the entire "Floral Classic" with water.

2. Using wire cutters, clip all the stems to seven inches.

3. Dip the flower stems in clear fingernail polish to seal the metal and prevent rusting.

4. Place three stems in each vase.

5. Put the four-vase unit in the center and add a three vases unit to each side. Add a tapered andle to the top vase for that extra special event.

Silk flowers we have chosen are orange ranuculus, yellow zinnias and variegated maidenhair fern.

1. Use all three units of your "Floral Classic."
2. Fill all the vases with small birdseed.
3. Cut all the stems eight inches in length.
4. Place one ranuculus into each vase and position the flowers to be upright in the birdseed.
5. Add one zinnia to each vase.
6. Fill with variegated maidenhair fern.

1. Use all three units of your "Floral Classic."
2. Fill all the vases with a funnel with hominy grits.
3. Cut all the artificial branches to nine inches.
4. Place one stem in every vase and arrange the branches to look like a tree.
5. Add your favorite Christmas ornaments, candy canes and small bows.

To create this fresh flower arrangement during your holiday season, simply use, red miniature carnations, white spider cushion mums and holly. All these flowers last well and look very festive for all your holiday occasions.

1. Use your entire "Floral Classic" set.
2. Fill your vases with water.
3. Cut all your flowers to seven inches in length.
4. Add two or three white spider mums to each vase.
5. Add two or three red miniature to each vase.
6. Fill in with variegated holly berry. Watch out for those leaves!
7. Place the four-vase unit in the center and slide one three-vase unit on each side.

If you have an evening affair, instead of flowers in the top vase, add a tapered candle to the center vase.

Red and White variegated roses with leather leaf fern. A beautiful fresh arrangement made easily!

1. Stack the entire "Floral Classic" set together.

2. Fill your vases with water.

3. Cut all your roses to seven inches. Make sure that they are cut and immediately placed in water. This will help keep the freshness of the rose.

4. Add leather leaf fern to fill in and prop up the rose. Enjoy!

This arrangement is so simple to make and anyone would enjoy having this as a gift. Use white spider cushion mums, red miniature carnations, and holly berry. Tis the season....

1. Use your entire "Floral Classic" set.

2. Cut all your flowers to seven inches in length.

3. Place two or three red miniature carnations in each vase. Make sure and use the buds too.

4. Add two or three white spider cushion mums to each vase.

5. Fill in with holly berry. You may use silk holly if fresh is not available. Just make sure and seal the bottom of the stem with clear fingernail polish so the wire will not rust.

1. Use just one three-vase unit and fill with water.
2. Fill each vase with a cluster of parsley.
3. Cut a hole in the top of your bell pepper and then place it in the cent or the three-vase unit.
4. Poke 1/4 of the toothpick into the top of the shrimp allowing the tail of the shrimp to hang out.
5. Put the toothpick through the parsley and place some of the shrimp with the toothpick into the pepper.
6. Add your favorite spicy cocktail sauce to the inside of the pepper and garnish with two or three sprigs of parsley.

Make up another pepper with shrimp for another appetizer in the other three-vase unit.

Create this delicious fruit appetizer for any occasion. You will need a large grapefruit, parsley and fruit kabobs of strawberries, grapes, and cantaloupe. Watch this one magically disappear.

1. Use one three-vase unit and fill with water.
2. Place a large grapefruit in the center of the vases.
3. Make fruit kabobs out of red and green grapes, cantaloupe strawberries.
4. Poke the kabobs onto the grapefruit and a kabob through the parsley.

You can also make a fruit dip of cream cheese and powdered sugar.

This always is a big hit at any party or holiday occasion. To prepare this delight, you will need a large red onion, white, brown and wheat bread, assorted lunch meats, cheese, olives, sweet pickles, and parsley. People will think that you hired a professional caterer for this appetizer.

1. Use one three-vase unit and fill with water.
2. Fill the vases with parsley clusters.
3. Use a canopy sandwich maker and alternate your breads, cheeses and lunchmeats for each one.
4. Attach pickles with a toothpick and place into the onion.
5. Add sandwiches.
6. Garnish with tomatoes and olives on the top of the skewers.

Notes